SARAH PALIN

POISED TO BECOME AMERICA'S FIRST FEMALE PRESIDENT

Recaldo Ochoa

Acknowledgements

When I started this project, a few friends spurred me on after they read the first few chapters. I am grateful and thankful to Virginia Wolfe and Diane Brown. I must extend special thanks also to Lisa Brown for her constructive suggestions on content and structure. I would also like to thank the following personnel from BookSurge for their invaluable contributions in bringing this book to print: my publishing consultant, David Beckman; my editorial services coordinator, Abby Harris; my editor, Gail Cato; and my account managers—Amanda Dunne-Porter, Lauren Mendenhall, Jeanne McNutt, April Owens, and Meredith Severs.

This book was a family collaborative effort—all members of my family contributed. My elder son, Wade, utilized his creative computer graphic and photo-editing skills for the book's front and back covers and many of the images inside. My daughter, Adel, created artistic and realistic pencil drawings of the Palins that really enhance the pages of this book. I am thankful to Jerron, my younger son, who added his artistic touch to one drawing and has been unwavering in his support and encouragement.

I am most thankful to my wife, Marianna, whose encouragement and love have been invaluable to me in making this work possible. She also took the time to read and edit the manuscript—fully participating in the development of this book.

To God I give the glory.

CONTENTS

Introduction

It was August 29 in Dayton, Ohio—a battleground state in the 2008 presidential election. An excited crowd waving American flags had gathered at high noon to see whom Senator John McCain, the Republican presidential candidate, would unveil as his vice presidential running mate. These Republican faithful wanted McCain to choose someone from within the party's conservative base, but no such person was reportedly on his immediate list of vice presidential prospects. Yet, they remained on high alert with great anticipation that they were about to witness a defining moment in the presidential campaign.

Meanwhile, Americans around the country and the world also waited in suspense, glued to their televisions sets, computers, or radios for McCain's revelation. It was now nearly six months since becoming the Republican presidential nominee and three days before the Republican National Convention, yet McCain had not revealed the individual who would be joining the ticket—it was long overdue.

The news media were predicting that it could be any of four men who were on John McCain's short list of potential running mates, including Senator Joe Lieberman of Connecticut; Governor Tim Pawlenty of Minnesota; Tom Ridge, former governor of Pennsylvania; and Mitt Romney, former governor of Massachusetts. However, McCain's maverick streak meant that nothing was off the table, including having a conservative or a woman on his ticket.

To everyone's surprise, McCain introduced the little-known governor of Alaska, Sarah Louise Palin, as his running mate. She ascended the stage with brisk, authoritative steps, followed by her husband and four of her five children amid thunderous applause. Dressed in an all-black, long-sleeved, straight-skirted suit with an American flag pin on her left collar, she looked more like a beauty queen than the mother of five. Palin exuded confidence, passion, and hope. She waved to the excited crowd with a trusting smile and a reassuring look through designer glasses, her hazel eyes mirroring the color of her insubordination. Sarah rehired Emmons the next day after strong press and public support for Emmons emerged; she agreed to place the library and the museum under her jurisdiction. Police Chief Irl Stambaugh did not enjoy the same fate. Feeling that he was fired because he opposed the new mayor's support on weapon concealment rights and her backing for bars to remain open during regular business hours, Stambaugh filed suit. But the court threw out his case because it concluded that the mayor acted within the scope of her authority and power. Sarah replaced Stambaugh with Charlie Fannon. Sarah knew that winning an election did not guarantee easy implementation of her election promises; she needed the full support of Wasilla's department heads. To ensure that department heads complied with her administrative policies and that she had the expertise to run Wasilla's city government, Sarah prudently created a city manager position for which she hired John Cramer. Cramer assisted the new mayor in managing and expanding the services and infrastructure of the city of Wasilla.

During her first term as mayor of Wasilla, Sarah accomplished a great deal to win the hearts of her constituents. Sarah gave a personal phone call to at least one resident of Wasilla every day to inquire about his or her well-being and to find out how the city was doing. She pulled these names out of a jar she had on her desk that contained all the names of Wasilla residents. She immediately took a pay cut of $4,000, reducing her annual salary from $68,000 to $64,000. Satisfied that the 2 percent sales tax Wasilla's residents were paying was sufficient to cover the cost of running the city, she reduced property taxes by 75 percent and removed all personal property and business inventory taxes.

Sarah Palin also improved and expanded the City of Wasilla's infrastructure to enhance the quality of life for its residents to accommodate the ever-increasing population of Wasilla. She was able to finance new infrastructure projects and expand funding for the police department by issuing city bonds. She protected fresh water from possible storm water contamination by treating the water before it entered the rivers and lakes. And to allow her constituents and visitors to enjoy more of Wasilla' beautiful outdoors, Sarah built a walk and bike path. She also saved Wasilla's taxpayers millions of dollars by halting construction on a new library and city hall.

The people of Wasilla were so pleased with Sarah's accomplishments during her first term in office; they elected her for a second term as their mayor by a 74 percent margin over former mayor and opponent John Stein. In recognition of her success and leadership,

Mayor Sarah Palin was elected president of the Alaska Conference of Mayors.

As an ardent sports enthusiast and fan, the second-term mayor achieved her most ambitious project yet—the $14.7 million Wasilla Multi-Use Sports Complex—by increasing sales taxes by a mere 0.5 percent. Although questions surfaced about the city's acquisition of and compensation for the land on which the complex was constructed, the complex was built on time and within budget—a testament to her fiscal conservatism.

Sarah knew that for Wasilla to grow and develop at the same pace of its population, it would require an infusion of monies beyond local collection and state allotments. Consequently, as mayor of Wasilla, she sought earmarks from the federal government by hiring Robertson, Monagle & Eastaugh to lobby for the city. With additional help from Steven Silver, the former chief of staff of Alaska's then senator Ted Stevens, the city of Wasilla received over $26 million in earmarks for projects such as sewer repair, the building of a new youth center, improving public transportation, and the building of a new railroad and a ski resort.

1-07-08

Chapter 7

Making a Difference

Unable to run for mayor of Wasilla for a third time because of term limits, Palin campaigned for the Republican nomination of lieutenant governor in 2002 at the age of thirty-eight. She ran against five Republican candidates and came in a strong second to Loren Leman who went on to win the state election. Although she lost this race, Sarah won the hearts and respect of most Alaskans who got to know her better because of the personal connections she made with them during the campaign; they began to view her as a fighter for their common good. She also gained the respect and admiration of Frank Murkowski, the former Alaska Republican senator and newly elected governor. Governor Murkowski appointed Palin a commissioner on the Alaska Oil and Gas Conservation Commission. She became chair for this commission and officiated in the capacity of ethics supervisor from 2003 to 2004.

Appalled by the apathetic and unethical conduct of one of her fellow Republicans on the commission and the indifference of Governor Murkowski to deal effectively with the issue, Sarah Palin resigned from the AOGCC in January, 2004. She subsequently made formal complaints against two of the highest-ranking Republicans in Alaska, namely, Republican Party head Randy Ruedrich, who served as a paid commissioner on the Alaska Oil and Gas Conservation Commission, but neglected his duties on the commission in favor of party business. She also raised ethical questions about Gregg Renkes, Murkowski's close friend and former Alaska attorney general, for financial conflict of interest on a coal trade agreement he negotiated on behalf of the state government. Consequently, Ruedrich and Renkes resigned from their respective state positions and Renkes was ordered to pay a fine of $12,000.

Many saw as political suicide Sarah's unprecedented but principled move to turn in members of her own party, but Sarah Palin was willing to jeopardize her political career for the interests of regular Alaskans. Sarah immediately became more committed and determined to fight for Alaskans by reforming government. First Sarah needed to prepare herself for the next executive position where she could achieve the greatest change for the people of Alaska.

Sarah Palin laid low for the next year and a half before she made her next move. She considered running for the US Senate in 2004 but decided against it. Meanwhile, Sarah Palin decided to prepare herself and other Republican women for training to hold political office. She served as a director of a 527 organization called Ted Stevens Excellence in Public Service, Inc., from 2004 to 2005. In 2006, Sarah Palin announced her intention to run for the Republican nomination for governor of Alaska.

Chapter 12

The Inadequate Vetting of Palin

Is Governor Sarah Palin unintelligible as the liberal media and some of McCain's former aides would have us believe? Or is the McCain campaign culpable of incompetence and poor judgment in its vetting of Palin? It's likely the latter! What should the campaign have done before tossing her into the national political arena without adequate warning and preparation—stripping her of her prior confidence and natural intellectual spontaneity she had developed with the media since becoming mayor of Wasilla?

Recaldo Ochoa

When candidates are running for the presidency of the United States, the most important decision they make—that weighs heavily on the quality of their judgment and leadership—is their choice for vice president. Individuals on the long and short lists of prospects face an intense vetting process; the prospective vice presidential candidates endure thorough background checks that cover personal conduct, professional career, finances, and prior media coverage. Then candidates participate in one or more face-to-face interviews with the vetting team, not only to respond to the above but also to reveal their competence or incompetence in relevant disciplines. The objective here is to narrow the list to a single vice presidential candidate who offers the fewest character flaws, has the most complementary experience, possesses the highest competence to replace the president if necessary, and can best attract certain segments of American voters to help the ticket win the White House.

If McCain's team had thoroughly vetted Sarah Palin, they would have discovered—very early in McCain's lengthy six-month reign as the Republican presumptive nominee—that the Alaska governor had the exceptional leadership ability to attract the Republican base he needed to his campaign. They also would have discovered that Sarah Palin's unconventional path from hockey mom to Alaska governor was so intense and short, that she had little time to become well versed in national and international issues.

They could have easily remedied this shortcoming by providing a coaching team for the young, intelligent Republican rising star—if they had seriously considered her for the ticket. But McCain's last-minute, hasty selection of Sarah Palin, without implementing the basic tenets of the vetting process—coupled with the campaign's media paranoia that followed—left her immensely susceptible to making gaffes when they later unceremoniously fed her to the voracious national media.

John McCain had more than adequate time to properly vet and select his running mate. McCain had close to six months after clinching the Republican presidential nomination, from March 4, 2008, to August 29, 2008, when he announced his vice presidential choice, to examine, evaluate, and select his running mate. His opponent, Barack Obama, had less than three months to choose his vice presidential nominee, yet he managed to thoroughly vet people under consideration. The full extent of McCain's vetting of Sarah Palin was to have her fill out a questionnaire with seventy questions. McCain's unveiling of Sarah Palin as his number two person on the ticket was a last-minute gut decision rather than a choice based on good judgment.

McCain first met Sarah Palin during the National Governors Association convention held in Washington, DC, February 20-24, 2008, less than two weeks before he clinched the Republican presidential presumptive nomination (March 4, 2008). Palin made an indelible impression on McCain with her command of the issues of energy and government reform. He was delighted to discover that she was a political maverick, just like him, who had fought to root out wasteful spending and corruption in government.

Since that meeting, Sarah Palin had been on McCain's long and short lists of potential vice presidential running mates, but she never thought that McCain had her under serious consideration until a few days before the Republican convention, after advisers persuaded him that his first choice for vice president, probably Senator Joe Lieberman, would disenfranchise the Republican base. Cognizant that his Democratic rival, Barack Obama, did not choose—as many had expected— Senator Hillary Clinton who drew a commanding eighteen million votes in the primary, McCain had a sudden revelation of Palin's advantage on his ticket: she would excite the Republican base and attract Hillary's disappointed female supporters.

Therefore, six months after his first meeting with Palin, five days before he revealed her as his running

Alaska. She is not only a dynamic, magnetic leader; Palin is also a tough democratic leader who leads by listening to and weighing expert solutions to problems, and is not afraid to make up her own mind on what needs to be done or to implement her resolutions.

As a freshman city council member, Palin led the fight against fiscal waste and self-interest by Wasilla's elected officials. She evaluated Mayor Stein' justification for increasing his $68,000 a year salary against the limited taxpayers' resources and opposed it. In fact, when she became mayor in 1996, Palin shaved $4,000 off that sum reducing her salary to $64,000. She even impeded the formidable senior council member Nick Carney's plan to mandate that all Wasilla's households pay his company for garbage disposal. She voted on the issues in the context and interest of the people of Wasilla who elected her to serve.

Appalled by city officials' fiscal irresponsibility, Palin orchestrated a peaceful transfer of power in 1996 when she became the mayor of Wasilla. But Mayor Sarah Palin encountered strong opposition from the city's department heads, and her city council detractor, Nick Carney, was threatening to derail her new administration.

After a short intense evaluation and consultations with her mentors, the new mayor demanded loyalty and commitment to her new administrative agenda by having heads of city departments submit letters of resignation and resumes for reapplication for their current positions. One resigned; she fired two others, but rehired one of them; the rest retained their jobs but only after pledging their allegiance to the new administration. Palin quickly assumed full leadership of her administration as the new mayor of Wasilla.

In addition, Palin's election as mayor created two vacancies on the city council. Wasilla's charter required these seats be filled by a unanimous vote by the members of the city council. With stern opposition and determination to frustrate her efforts, Nick Carney stalled the selection of new council members. Mayor Sarah Palin, even without clear direction from city ordinance, threatened to make the appointments herself. Fearing that she would turn the tables on him by naming two handpicked allies caused Carney to capitulate, voting to fill the seats so that Palin could begin to fulfill her campaign promises to the residents of Wasilla.

Palin took full command of Wasilla's city government and, working with the council, she reduced property taxes and eliminated certain business taxes. The residents were so pleased with her leadership as mayor they elected her for a second term with 74 percent of the votes cast. She went on to expand Wasilla's infrastructure and built the city's first multi-sports complex.

Sarah Palin led the Alaska Oil and Gas Conservation Commission (AOGCC) as the chair and ethics supervisor for more than a year. There she clashed with top Republicans; she charged some with dereliction of duty and unethical business practices without concern for the repercussions it might have on her political career. When then Governor Frank Murkowski refused to act, she resigned, causing him to take action against the perpetrators. As a leader, Palin is not afraid to make tough decisions and stand to by them with integrity and fortitude.

Privy to the culture of partisanship, indifference, corruption, and special interest in the Alaska state government, Palin decided to lead a political revolt against the Murkowski administration in the 2006 gubernatorial election. Shunned by the Republican leadership, Sarah Palin launched a grassroots campaign that soon spread like wildfire among Alaskans—who had grown weary of politics as usual. She surged past Murkowski in the primary and crossed over the victory line with an army of Alaska voters pushing her ahead of her closest rival, Knowles, in the general election to take the highest position of leadership in the state of Alaska.

Recaldo Ochoa

She is an independent leader of leaders. She considers political leadership as a position of sacred trust bestowed by citizens upon politicians to perform public service with integrity and transparency, putting the interest of the people first. Voters should replace those who serve only their own self-interests disregarding taxpayers, with ethical leaders who address constituents' concerns.

Conclusion

She possesses the intelligence, the judgment, the moral character, the leadership, and the experience to confidently lead Americans into the twenty-first century. By 2012 and 2016, Sarah Palin will have brought twenty to twenty-four years of her political autobiography for Americans to scrutinize and weigh against other worthy contenders' resumes; hers is likely to remain strong and emerge as an unbeatable presidential package.

Sarah Palin is not the typical politician who entered public life because of political affiliations or a family legacy to fulfill personal ambitions or career goals. She got into politics to promote the interests of the people in her community and state by improving their lives and increasing their opportunities for prosperity. Instead of imposing her will on the people, she finds out what they want by listening and living among them; then she addresses their needs.

Consequently, she enjoys a more genuine interpersonal connectivity with people on a deeper non-verbal—emotional and intellectual—level than other politicians do. She sincerely identifies with the concerns and aspirations of average Americans. She's America's "Ms. Congeniality." Her sincerity radiates from her smile, her concerned look, her conversation, her tone, her deportment, her mannerisms, her handshake, and her ability to listen and respond appropriately.

Conclusion

But she also walks her talk. Sarah's word is her bond. She has a reputation for delivering on her promises as council member, mayor, and governor. She has proven to the people of Alaska that she is worthy of the trust they have placed in her. Within the next four to eight years, she will probably request and gain the confidence of the American people.

People are in awe of Palin's fearlessness. She will not acquiesce, even in the face of unprecedented opposition. She has challenged and defeated many political Goliaths on her journey to becoming governor of Alaska. Undaunted, she confronted the mayor of Wasilla, the governor of Alaska, and the Republican hierarchy, even when she was outnumbered or outgunned. She knows how to achieve victory against seasoned politicians, and fights for the American people.

Sometimes a person's rise to political leadership has as much to do with opportunity as with fitness and qualifications. This is Sarah Palin's time and she is in the ideal place in American history to become the *first female president* of the greatest nation on earth. America has elected its first African-American president and it is ready to elect its *first female president*. Palin is ready, willing, and able, at this time and in this place, to assume her next logical executive position—the presidency.

About the Author

Copyright © 2009 Wade Ochoa

Recaldo Ochoa is a high school teacher who has taken over three hundred of his students to the halls of Congress and the White House to experience their federal government in action. He teaches American history, US government, and world history. He is happily married with two sons and a daughter. He has a BA in psychology, an MA in history, and an MS in education.